Help Me Understand

Why Are Drugs and Alcohol Bad for Me?

Elizabeth Krajnik

PowerKiDS
press™

NEW YORK

Published in 2019 by The Rosen Publishing Group, Inc.
29 East 21st Street, New York, NY 10010

First Edition

Editor: Elizabeth Krajnik
Book Design: Rachel Rising

Photo Credits: Cover Evgeny Karandaev/Shutterstock.com; p. 4 monticello/Shutterstock.com; p. 5 Sherry Yates Young/Shutterstock.com; p. 7 Evdokimov Maxim/Shutterstock.com; p. 8 vandycan/Shutterstock.com; p. 9 Gorodenkoff/Shutterstock.com; p. 11 ANDREA DELBO/Shutterstock.com; p. 12 Boltenkoff/Shutterstock.com; p.13 Tunatura/Shutterstock.com; p. 15 Volodymyr Tverdokhlib/Shutterstock.com; p. 17 Jan H Andersen/Shutterstock.com; p. 19 FabrikaSimf/Shutterstock.com; p. 20 Africa Studio/Shutterstock.com; p. 21 Marko Aliaksandr/Shutterstock.com; p. 22 Fran Marin/Shutterstock.com.

Cataloging-in-Publication Data

Names: Krajnik, Elizabeth.
Title: Why are drugs and alcohol bad for me? / Elizabeth Krajnik.
Description: New York : PowerKids Press, 2019. | Series: Help me understand | Includes glossary and index.
Identifiers: LCCN ISBN 9781508167242 (pbk.) | ISBN 9781508167228 (library bound) | ISBN 9781508167259 (6 pack)
Subjects: LCSH: Drugs–Juvenile literature. | Alcohol–Juvenile literature. | Drug abuse–Juvenile literature. | Drug abuse–Prevention–Juvenile literature.
Classification: LCC RM301.K73 2019 | DDC 363.45–dc23

Manufactured in the United States of America

CPSIA Compliance Information: Batch #CS18PK: For Further Information contact Rosen Publishing, New York, New York at 1-800-237-9932

Contents

What Are Drugs and Alcohol?

A drug is a **substance** often used as a medicine or used to make medicines. These drugs can help us. But some drugs are harmful. These drugs are often illegal because they put people's lives in danger. However, even drugs that are legal can be harmful if used to get **high**.

Alcohol is the substance in drinks that can make a person drunk, but the word can also mean the drinks themselves. Alcohol is sometimes used in medicines and other products too. It's often considered a drug.

4

The drugs your doctor gives you and the ones you buy off the shelf at the store can be just as harmful as illegal drugs. Make sure you read the label carefully and take only the suggested amount after your parents have said it's OK.

Narcotics

Narcotics, or opioids, are a type of drug often given to people in hospitals to help treat pain. In many cases, people become **addicted** to these drugs, in part because they can make people feel less pain and **anxiety**.

Opioids can be very harmful. Some people overdose, or use too much of a drug, because they don't know how the drug will affect them. These overdoses sometimes lead to death. Narcotics are a controlled substance, which means they're illegal except in certain cases.

Heroin is a very harmful narcotic. Heroin use can cause people to become addicted. Heroin addicts often have a hard time getting off the drug.

⟶

Stimulants

Stimulants are drugs that increase how much energy a person has. Drugs such as Adderall and Ritalin are stimulants doctors give people to help them focus, or pay close attention to something.

However, all stimulants, including illegal drugs such as cocaine and methamphetamine, or meth, speed up the body's systems. This can be harmful because they increase a person's heart rate. This can cause an uneven heartbeat or cause a person's body to become far too hot.

blue meth →

Meth **laboratories** are very dangerous because the substances used to make meth are very flammable, or easily lit on fire. Meth labs can also **contaminate** their surroundings.

9

Hallucinogens

Hallucinogens are a type of drug that can change how you feel, hear, smell, taste, or see things. They can also change your mood. Some of these drugs occur naturally in plants and others are made in laboratories.

MDMA, commonly called ecstasy, often comes in pill form. This drug causes most people to feel very happy and connected to other people. However, it can be very dangerous because it also acts as a stimulant. It can cause heart issues, trouble remembering things, and other problems.

Some types of mushrooms contain a **chemical** called psilocybin, which can cause people to hallucinate, or see things that aren't really there. People may also have panic attacks or trouble telling what's real.

Marijuana

Marijuana is a name for the drug that comes from the *Cannabis sativa* plant. It's a psychoactive drug, which means that it affects a person's mind or behavior.

Even though marijuana is a legal drug in some states in the United States, it's still a controlled substance. Using marijuana can make people very sleepy or cause decreased blood pressure and increased appetite. Over a long period of time, using marijuana can cause lung problems and may cause people to get sick more often.

marijuana leaf →

Marijuana is a controlled substance. However, some **rehabilitation** facilities in states where marijuana is legal use it to help people addicted to other drugs and alcohol.

Anabolic Steroids

Steroids are chemicals our bodies produce naturally. However, people can also make steroids in a lab. Corticosteroids can help treat many problems and sicknesses. Anabolic steroids are controlled substances made in a lab. People sometimes use them to make their muscles grow and to help them perform better in sports.

Young adults who use anabolic steroids might grow less or more slowly. Young women who use anabolic steroids might get deeper voices or increased body and facial hair. They may even lose their hair.

Using anabolic steroids can increase the chances of a heart attack or a stroke. Steroids can also cause harm to a person's liver.

$\longrightarrow$

15

Inhalants

Some people use the chemical vapors from certain household products to get high. These types of drugs are called inhalants because users inhale, or breathe in, the vapor through their nose or mouth. Some common inhalants include glue, cleaning products, and paint thinner.

Using inhalants can cause a person to have trouble speaking clearly, trouble moving around, dizziness, and a feeling of great happiness. Inhalant use can also cause death. Over a long period of use, a person may have weight loss, trouble concentrating, and muscle weakness.

Sniffing inhalants again and again in a short period of time can kill a person because there's too much of the drug in their lungs and not enough oxygen to breathe.

Designer Drugs

Some people try to design, or make, and sell their own drugs. These drugs often have a slightly different chemical makeup but produce the same effects as controlled substances. Each class of drug can be made in a lab. However, some designer drugs are more common than others.

"Bath salts" are a type of synthetic, or lab-made, stimulant. The effects of bath salts are similar to those of cocaine, meth, and MDMA. K2 or "spice" are the names of synthetic drugs that have effects similar to those of marijuana.

Fentanyl, a synthetic opioid, is stronger than other opioids such as heroin and morphine. It's sometimes used as a medicine. However, people sometimes create substances much like fentanyl that are illegal and even more dangerous.

$\longrightarrow$

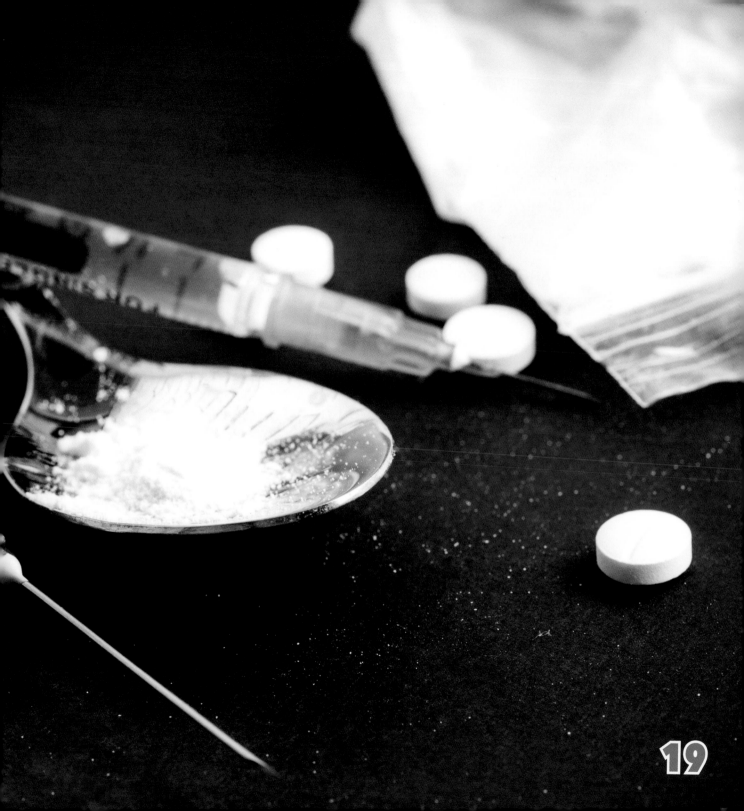

19

Depressants

Depressants are drugs that slow your body down, put you to sleep, prevent **seizures**, and help with anxiety. People can get legal depressants, such as barbiturates and benzodiazepines, from their doctors.

Some people use depressants to hurt others. GHB and Rohypnol are illegal drugs in the United States. They may be a liquid or white powder. People sometimes mix these drugs into drinks. They can make the user feel good and calm, but they may also cause people to lose consciousness. They may forget what happened while they were on the drug.

Alcohol is a depressant. In the United States, it's legal for people 21 years old and older to purchase alcohol. However, if a person drinks too much alcohol, their body can slow down so much that they might need to go to the hospital. They may even die.

21

Stay Safe

Some drugs help us get better when we're sick. However, unless a doctor says you should take a certain drug, you should try your hardest to stay away from them. Drugs and alcohol can be very harmful to your body.

A friend or even a stranger might say that taking drugs or drinking alcohol makes you feel good and can be fun. However, their effects on your body aren't worth the high. Saying no to drugs makes you a very strong person.

Glossary

addicted: Unable to stop doing something, which can lead to health problems.

anxiety: Fear or nervousness about what might happen.

chemical: Matter that can be mixed with other matter to cause changes.

contaminate: To make unfit for use by adding something harmful or unpleasant.

high: A state of intoxication, or lessened control over one's body or mind, produced by drugs or alcohol.

laboratory: A room or building in which people do scientific experiments and tests; also a place in which people make drugs in secret.

rehabilitation: The act of bringing someone back to a normal, healthy condition after an illness or addiction.

seizure: A sudden attack of uncontrollable movements, such as extreme twitching of muscles, caused by abnormal brain activity.

substance: A certain kind of material, or matter.

Index

Websites

Due to the changing nature of Internet links, PowerKids Press has developed an online list of websites related to the subject of this book. This site is updated regularly. Please use this link to access the list: www.powerkidslinks.com/help/alcohol